Praise for *Pleasure P*

"Beneath the understated precision of Mad
an electric current of desire—for truth, to
dered with archetypal, psychic potency. A pared sound is pierced
by an embodied, epiphanic wisdom, how 'one could die without
knowing this / the wild heart of all objects.' Poems written in the
ruins. Afterlives. And, everywhere, something dark and gorgeous
and burning inside the words."

—Aracelis Girmay, author of *the black maria*

"In Madeleine Cravens's *Pleasure Principle*, a tough particular-
ness operates perfectly in tandem with a subtle musicality and a
relentlessness of vision, a commitment to saying what has been
experienced just as it was experienced, and what has been imag-
ined as if it had been experienced. And yet these are also poems
that acknowledge the world as governed by possibility as much
as by pattern—when Cravens writes, 'There was a world inside
the world. I wanted the hard pit,' she is writing her way toward
a possible world, the world in the seed in the world. This book
is itself such a seed, both the beginning of a poet and a renewal
of poetry."

—Shane McCrae, author of *Pulling the Chariot of the Sun*

"Madeleine Cravens's *Pleasure Principle* draws the world with
an astounding clarity of vision, yet every setting is infused with
tenderness. These are taut and quiet poems, driven by an exhil-
arating lyric sensibility. The book begins where a photograph
would end—her lines hum with the frequency of unseen light,
hidden desires, forgotten objects, and memories retrieved from
the mystery of childhood. A truly wonderful debut announcing a
poet assured of her voice."

—Aria Aber, author of *Hard Damage*

PLEASURE PRINCIPLE

POEMS

MADELEINE CRAVENS

Scribner

New York   London   Toronto   Sydney   New Delhi

Scribner
An Imprint of Simon & Schuster, LLC
1230 Avenue of the Americas
New York, NY 10020

First Scribner trade paperback edition June 2024

Scribner and design are trademarks of Simon & Schuster, LLC.

Simon & Schuster: Celebrating 100 Years of Publishing in 2024

For information about special discounts for bulk purchases,
please contact Simon & Schuster Special Sales at 1-866-506-1949
or business@simonandschuster.com.

The Simon & Schuster Speakers Bureau can bring authors to your live event.
For more information, or to book an event, contact the Simon & Schuster Speakers
Bureau at 1-866-248-3049 or visit our website at www.simonspeakers.com.

Interior design by Davina Mock-Maniscalco

Manufactured in the United States of America

10 9 8 7 6 5 4 3 2 1

Library of Congress Cataloging-in-Publication Data:

Names: Cravens, Madeleine, 1995– author.
Title: Pleasure principle : poems / Madeleine Cravens.
Other titles: Pleasure principle (Compilation)
Description: First Scribner trade paperback edition. | New York : Scribner, 2024.
Identifiers: LCCN 2023055137 (print) | LCCN 2023055138 (ebook) |
    ISBN 9781668037768 (trade paperback) | ISBN 9781668037775 (ebook)
Subjects: LCGFT: Poetry.
Classification: LCC PS3603.R3945 P57 2024 (print) | LCC PS3603.R3945 (ebook) |
    DDC 811/.6—dc23/eng/20231214
LC record available at https://lccn.loc.gov/2023055137
LC ebook record available at https://lccn.loc.gov/2023055138

ISBN 978-1-6680-3776-8
ISBN 978-1-6680-3777-5 (ebook)

For Meg

I want to write to you like someone learning.

—Clarice Lispector
(translated by Stefan Tobler)

CONTENTS

III

PLEASURE PRINCIPLE

LEAVING

Not the pleasure of lovers but the pleasure of letters,
a pleasure like weather, delayed and prepared for,
not the pleasure of lessons but the pleasure of errors,
of nightmares, of actors in the black box of a theater,
not the pleasure of present but the pleasure of later,
the pleasure of letters and weather and terror, asleep
by the lake, unable to answer, the pleasure of candles,
their wax on the table, not the pleasure of saviors
but the pleasure of errors, not the pleasure of marriage
but the pleasure of failure, the pleasure of characters
like family members, their failures and errors, their
laughter and weather, the pleasure of water, terrible
rivers, not the pleasure of empire but the pleasure
of after, our failure to keep an accurate record, not
the pleasure of tethers but the pleasure of strangers,
the terrible strangers who will become your lovers,
not the pleasure of novels but the pleasure of anger,
your failure to answer all of my letters, the pleasure
of daughters, the pleasure of daughters writing letters
in April, the failure of orchards, the terror of mothers,
not the pleasure of planners but the pleasure of errors.

I

OBJECT PERMANENCE

I want to know how things will end. I've heard of the beginning,
how grains of pollen fell from the poplars. Then a little choral

music, cavalry, bright skirmish on the hillside, a thousand
years of this. Here is a flute and here is a steamship. Here is a gun

and your grandmother's ring. The devil has seven blue heads,
and when we draw him on the inside of the chapel, each one

tells a different lie. How many gods do you believe in?
How many good men? The story of the world can be told

in relation to umbrellas, invented in the seventh century
when we finally had enough rain. Don't look at the gun

directly. And don't remove the flute from its sheath of ice.
The end's already in motion, the end was starting this whole

time and today Brooklyn is a beautiful, devastating autumn.
Everyone I love is dancing in the plaza. A band plays below

the archway, we're drinking wine and rolling up our sleeves
to show the soft parts of our arms. When this ends I hope

it ends completely. How brave I feel, right now, watching
my old friends beside my father and imagining the end

as one imagines something certain, a birthday or a doctor's
visit. Not like last year when we watched the movie about

ruins—I ignored the crusted amphitheater and wanted
to touch you. It was February. You wore a long blue coat.

INHERITANCE

Inside the house, we said our names, and loved
each other in the historic way, with bartering
and harsh alliances. We slept soundly on the train
as it moved through stations, somehow waking
exactly at our stop. Outside the house: five eggs
frying in the diner, manta rays at the aquarium, green
parrots roosting in the cemetery. Outside the house:
hill good for sledding, hill bad for sledding, deep
hole where towers were. Inconvenient dumpster fire.
Branches after female hurricane. Each day came
without permission, in collections of old subway
tokens, cracked-open rose quartz, a certain hidden
Polaroid of parents newly married in Grand Central.
Dumb looks of shock. It must be summer because
they're sweating, astrological blue ceiling blinking
in alarm but the background crowd unbothered—
hordes of people eating, leaving, or returning
home, and arriving far too late, I know, but with
offers of repentance, coffee, fresh bodega flowers.

NARRATIVE

Once, my father told my sister and me a story
about an overturned fruit cart, a mountainous village.
In my sister's memory, an old woman chased after oranges.
The mayor of the village watched her and laughed.
Obstacles must separate characters from their desires:
this is called plot. The old woman wanted the fruit
and the terrain of the village created a barrier.
If we had trusted each other, we would have
been honest, able to confirm our parents' flaws.
You hated to be touched as a child, my sister said.
In my memory, there was no causality. There were not
even characters. Only oranges cascading down a hillside.

COASTAL RESILIENCY

My father studied superstorms.
He spread the flood map on the table,
named the neighborhoods that could be gone
in one hundred years. *Red Hook. Brighton
Beach. The Rockaways.* When the hurricane
arrived in late October, his girlfriend
swept dead leaves off their car. My mother
waded through the basement to retrieve
his files, and Ariana kissed me on the bridge,
then slept with Brandon after everyone
downtown lost power. Our high school
filled with foul water. In May, the oak trees
on Houston rotted. The Parks Department
took out their chainsaws.

PROVINCETOWN

Rachel says I have a hungry ghost inside me.
That my generation doesn't know our own history.
By the harbor, men walk together in muscular pairs
and for some reason all I think about is death—
death at the maritime cemetery, death
at the dispensary with gangly adolescents,
death at the sex shop where I run my hands
over the harnesses and leave, purchasing
nothing. Death as dusk hits clapboard houses.
I thought by twenty-seven I'd stop searching
for the story, as if stories were simultaneous
with action, rather than events recollected
incorrectly, rife with holes. My character wades
waist-deep in the bay, waiting for a revelation.
I want the plot to start here, at the end
of the two-lane highway, and then in the moon-
like dunes, the scrubby grass we trudged through.

SAPPHIC FRAGMENT

I didn't like sex in the beginning.
Somewhere in Greece, the sea eroded rocks.
There was no oracle. Spring lambs roasted

on wooden spits, sending a charred scent
into inland towns, smoke gathering on rooftops.
I had been lied to. Women, too, were violent.

The presidential candidate praised drones.
My sister was in the psychiatric hospital.
My mother kept repainting the kitchen.

Burnt orange, lime green. A dirty sort of gold.
In the nightclub bathroom, I inhaled strange
vapors, then smashed my head into a wall.

PLEASURE PRINCIPLE

After the party, Ellen choked me against the refrigerator.
It was very quiet. Other students filtered into the snow.

Can there be a story where a character wants nothing?
Even in happiness I did not find much satisfaction.

Or was it the other way around, little crushed-up pills,
desire requiring more desire, streetlights, cruel fields.

Sweet post-nasal drip. Years unwound quickly.
With the momentum of bargains and cold calculations,

destruction could be shaped into a mode of preservation.
I cut my hand on a mirror. A blonde nurse burned it shut.

BEIRUT

Mornings, I watched groups of runners
from my balcony. A one-eyed cat roamed
the street below. My neighbors all had purple shutters
strung together with steel wire. I had one friend.
Outside the city, we found a mill abandoned
on a hillside, its thresher oxidized by mist.
A goat charged at us with bared teeth.
There was often the problem of electricity.
I bought a space heater and set it near
my bed, which stood on wooden
risers. At the edge, I waited. Then it
was winter, a word synonymous with rain.
I understood less of any language by the day.
When we pulled off the highway to walk
through the valley, I heard a young boy
singing, but saw only his mother.

And when I visited another city, in the north,
I arrived just as the famous market closed.
At dusk, a sudden rolling down of curtains.
I dreamed about my sister in Cleveland.
We still weren't speaking. The year spun out
from under me, a rush of jasmine, vocal
traffic. How I repeated to myself or anyone—
a nun, a repairman who had come
to fix my sink—I live here.

ROAD TO HARISSA

Maryam drove too fast
through the mountains. Look, she said,
it's Jesus, as we passed the figure on the hill,
but it was actually the Virgin Mary,
arms raised in benediction. The week
after Easter was called Bright Week,
and Behbod was obsessed with a line
from Dante: *we were sullen in the sweet
air.* He repeated this while drinking
his green bottles of Almaza Beer
as we watched the processionals,
nuns with half-gone candles, small girls
weaving between them. When Israeli
jets bombed a power plant, an oily sheen
appeared on the sea.

ROAD TO BYBLOS

Mechanized time
was an invention created
to sustain entire empires.

And love, I knew, could be expressed
through an idiom about graves.

We rode past the beachside
nightclub and three
cement factories.

I wasn't in love.
I never knew what time it was.

Smoke unfurled from the air base.
A pregnant dog howled
under a fig tree.

VOICEMAIL FROM LA JOLLA

I wanted to learn your California theories.
The false collective of the freeway,
time unspooled from units. It didn't seem
like something I could figure out intuitively:
how the past penetrates the present,
and present flows back into the past.
Amniotic pulse of traffic. Erotic blush
of bougainvillea. My best friends
at their beachside weddings. Three
dead sea lions at Solana Beach, swollen
but intact. Womanhood felt like an incorrect
container for the kind of life I was pursuing.
But it also might have been the general future
which appeared ill-fitting. You didn't pick up.
I walked out to the Pacific, crouched
beside a tide pool to prod a sea anemone.
It clenched around my finger.

BODEGA BAY

We watched a movie about
an orchestral conductor, a powerful
woman who groomed young musicians.
I didn't understand the ending.
Driving to the beach, it began to rain.

Red cattle stood slack-jawed on the hill
by the ravine. I like cows, you said.
They're the most generous animal.

We fought about that for a little.
The difference between giving and being
used. To our left, there was some sort of prayer circle.
The leader wore a hat shaped like a pinecone.
Unobtrusively, the moon rose.

We talked about your other lover on the long ride
home. The rain started up again. Again
I tried to free my mind.

POINT REYES

It was late June, the solstice.
The day took hours to end. You look like me,
my father said quietly. We stood by the San Andreas Fault.
Soon, the plates would shift, toppling multiple
cities. But the rift wasn't visible; a bay
covered the fissure. We rested our arms
on the railing as the sky debased itself. Pink
leaking into gold, gold reflected on dark water,
a lesser version, a replica.

THE FEAST OF SAINT FRANCIS

The cattle lower their heads
as they enter the chapel. Even the lowly
will be anointed. Because Francis too
had his time in the wilderness, lost in the mountains
outside Assisi. He was drunk for months.
Coming down from the hillside, he kissed
a man out of pity, and through this grace
became sainted. I'm missing part of the story:
the kiss was likely a test. And only briefly
have I understood sublimity, walking through
Central Park the morning after I met you.
I had to go to the dentist. But I paused
for the horses, beautiful and humiliated.
Cardinal in my rib cage, a thin silver ringing.
Look. I am trying to remember animals.
To picture my city's yearly processional.
The hand of the priest on the back of the camel
and the dead rat outside the cathedral.
The sick man at the foot of the mountain,
waiting for anyone to come down.

HOMECOMING

I exit the music hall
to a corrupted winter. The air thick with evidence.
A hand or its shadow. Sediment of the moon.
Brooklyn is a crypt of girlhood
and I must attempt to love it—
to circumvent the pain point. Keep shut
the red box of letters. Late December.
Confetti on the pavement. East River slow,
nearly frozen. What I took to be the termination
of the growing season, no tries left
for newness.

II

DESIRE LINES

1.

I live above a vet.
You live above a florist. Drunk
in the daytime, I hate to see cats tucked
in bags. Cut flowers placed in the window.

You live near my father.
He used to say the city's parks were not
in competition. Though he did point out
that Prospect Park was built second—

so the man who planned it,
Olmsted, had more time to practice. To mimic
the British pastoral, drawing two concentric
circles, carving a pond between artificial hills.

Tonight, in Brooklyn, my father plans his second
wedding. Considers the music and flowers.
At the end, they will own each other.
This is perfectly normal.

2.

After we met,
I sent you a picture of my naked body.
Good girl, you said, and something inside me shifted,
came unhinged.

3.

Running up Olmsted's hill,
I wonder if I am more or less in pain
than other strangers. Young mothers push babies
in strollers. I wake before dawn and vomit.

Strings of mist gather at the pond's edge,
like certain nineteenth century landscape paintings.

In my anxiety, a rush of objectivity.
Longing has its own economy. Boats tied up
in the water. Carriage horses, pairs of swans—

throughout my childhood, my father
pointed to the footpaths that bisected the grass.
Shortcuts, rejections of the planner's hand.
Desire lines, he called them.

4.

Another frantic September.
The arch meets the plaza. The plaza feeds
into the park. By the boathouse, Joe and I watch
two racoons pull a chicken wing from the trash.

I've been thinking about how Melanie Klein
described the depressive position. A circuit, an urge
toward repair.

5.

Let me begin again.
Coming back from the nightclub. The hum
of the ceiling fan, pigeons brutally cooing.

This whole thing makes me feel sick, you said.
Like I'm doing something I shouldn't.

I looked out your window
and examined my city. The blue domed roof
of the synagogue. My father waking up across
the street, my mother on the other side
of the plaza.

6.

Last night, a pit bull bit
a woman at one end of the meadow.
A man came over and hit the dog on the head
with a stick, but still, the dog didn't let go.

Olmsted meant for it to feel like this. Movement
toward action, no real completion or arrival.

Like how at your door, I wanted to be in your room.
In your room, I wanted to see inside your skin.
Your husband was away, in San Francisco.

You picked up my palm and pretended
to read it. You will live a long life, you said.
Just kidding.

7.

Joe says I shouldn't apologize for my obsessions;
they're entertaining.

8.

December. The mechanics
on Atlantic are preparing for snow.
I call the hotline with a theoretical question.

The man who answers tells me to make time
for pleasure. How can I tell him I am tired

of pleasure. I want to live quietly, beyond
cities, their histories, the need for parks
and architecture, oak trees hanging low
over the service road—

9.

Two teenage girls are drunk
on Smirnoff by the waterfall, blowing smoke
into each other's faces. I hear one scream
don't ever leave me.

10.

Waiting is a way of not feeling, Joe says.

11.

I know melancholia is a kind of fixation.

Other runners are the only people here today.
We haul ourselves up the frozen hill, choking
on cold air, as if it were a punishment.

My father always used to say, you don't lose
things, Madeleine, you just misplace them—.

Olmsted, too, loved contradictions.
He wanted the park to contain human spectacle,
and also, as a stretch of emptiness, to suggest
what happens after.

12.

A prospect is a point on the horizon—

13.

Three days after my father
left my mother, the four of us took the train
into Manhattan to meet with a psychologist.
After, we walked through the larger park,
the famous one. We found a public art exhibit along
the concrete paths: thousands of orange gates
strung with orange fabric.

14.

Near the park's northern entrance,
a woman is hurling objects from the window
of her parked car at a man who is standing on the sidewalk,
apologizing. She throws a flip-flop, an apple,
some magazines.

15.

My mother and I had a game, too.
Each fall, we would count the Japanese maples,
distinct because of their jagged leaves. I never loved
him, I remember her saying, just once,
as we crossed the plaza.

16.

The border between winter
and spring, the precipice. The trees betray
new leaves. I decide I like the southern edge
of the park best, by the freeway and the cemetery,
the Victorian mansions of Ditmas.

A team of girls in cleats circles the softball fields,
practicing. For no reason, a man starts to juggle.

Skaters trace the plaza, trying to jump the curb.

Last night I let a stranger hit me in the face.
She was a therapist. After, we discussed real estate.
Proximity to green space, the price
of natural light.

17.

I have all my life considered distance, wrote Olmsted.

18.

Like you, my father was a photographer.

19.

By the drummer's grove,
Joe says I should stop. That Baudrillard
thought running was a kind of preparation for death,
one more way of perfecting the body
for embalmment.

20.

I left Brooklyn at twenty.
I fell in love for the first time. There was
an element of terror when she removed her rings.
I could be shaped, I could be changed,
I could see a future and be denied it—.

When I used to kiss men, I felt nothing.
Only their total inability to annihilate me.

21.

I find your loneliness
very honest, you said to me, the night we met.
We sat in the plaza by the copper statue
of Neptune. And then you looked at me
sort of sadly and said, you're so young.

After, we walked to the park, jumped over
the low stone wall.

22.

You told me the word *remote*
comes from botany. I think about this as I sprint
through the tunnel, toward Flatbush Avenue.
A man is playing saxophone by the Camperdown elm,
a small crowd surrounding him. Of all my characters,
I enjoyed your company the most.

III

AT THE ASHOKAN WATERSHED

Water travels ninety-three miles
to get to the city. I understand the process
now that I am not allowed abstractions.
Bald eagles nest here. Rainbow trout swim.
Too much, you said, regarding what I wanted.
It was a question of resources and scarcity.
One could try to believe in abundance,
but there was so much evidence in favor
of the opposite: depletion, chaos, loss.
Now the sun breaks over the spillway.
I make you plain in my imagination, plain
and obvious.

IN THE CATSKILLS

Beside the house, in the last
uncovered field, neighbors build a new stone wall
from pieces of the older one. There's a rush
to finish by December. At night, I hear you
calling him. You're reading Yeats
again, "The Wild Swans at Coole."

I wake to dead hydrangeas beating
against the windowpane. At lunch, you finally
speak, saying something about Yeats
and Maude. The dog skirts the pond
and won't come near me even if I'm whistling.
The deer stay at the top of the hill, unaware
of the platforms there, built into the trees.
I think of all the times I displayed my body—
in the movie theater, in the hotel bar.
There was a red shirt you liked me
to wear. Stupid Yeats. Stupid Maude.
Stupid dog each day bounding from the car.

POLYAMORY

Originally, I wanted the story
to have several female characters.
I thought it would be better
to be untethered to one perspective,
that a chorus would strengthen
the plot.

But I couldn't accept the inverse.
At heart, I wanted to be possessed.

Last night, in Hudson,
L spoke to me in her father's language,
the language of my favorite novel.
It seemed like she was naming parts
of my body, though I couldn't be sure.

Does translation eliminate music?
In the weak light I climbed
on top of her.

THE PHOTOGRAPHER

We sat in the narrow plaza filled
with metal tables by the construction site.
It was warm, around five p.m., one of those
evenings after a long winter where
the city seemed to be anxiously flowering.
Several acquaintances rode by on bicycles.
There was a line outside the pharmacy
on Fulton where they yelled everyone's
full name and then their medication.
Soon you would travel to another state
to take pictures of a famous dancer.
You think it's about honesty, you said,
but it's not, it's about staging,
also light. Behind you, two floors up,
I could see into my room. The little vases
on the windowsill looked pathetic, girlish,
so carefully arranged.

NATURAL HISTORY

Uptown, we visit the shark exhibit.
To Be Great Is to Be Misunderstood.
Infant sharks swim in formaldehyde as the scientist's
recorded voice explains the randomness of survival.
Yesterday someone opened fire on the N train.
Today Central Park is full of daffodils, a carousel
of horses in positions of submission. Each rider
plays the role of conqueror. I didn't want
to come here. I wanted to go to the planetarium.
To stand on the scale that shows your weight on Mars.
To forget our brief arrangement. To consider
what might lie beyond this, what might live
outside this life.

LAUREL CANYON WEDDING

Tonight I'm speeding past the date palms,
the wispy hills like the heads of blonde infants.
Behind me, a party where little pieces of meat
were served on silver trays and the groom's
mother cried, describing him as a boy.
And then said, now you belong to your wife.
And everyone raised their champagne flutes.
And I looked across the patio at the bartender
and saw that she was looking at me, and we both
looked away, and a drone flew above us, capturing
the night, creating an archive. And the bride
closed her eyes and threw a bouquet behind her,
toward a row of thin-armed women in pink.
Actually, at first, the bride only pretended.
And the women jumped and landed, empty-handed.
I remembered how my sister and I would trick our dog
like this, mimicking throwing the ball but at the last
moment holding onto it, so that the dog would run
far into the meadow, after nothing.

5 NORTH

Between Los Angeles and Oakland,
there was snow on the grass-covered mountains,
which made a strange pattern, like brushstrokes
on paper. Then the mountains gave way
to the flatness of farms. At a rest stop near Fresno,
a beautiful woman spat into a cup. Orange trees
blurred into feedlots. The sheep weren't
upsetting but the cows were horrific, acres
of them behind concrete walls. They slept,
resigned to their pens. Across the road
were several withered rows of almond groves.
And a sign, *Congress Created the Dust Bowl.*
Wind cut through the valley, pushed the trucks
toward the median. For a while, I felt guilty,
and then the feeling lifted.

JACOB RIIS BEACH

Behind the decrepit hospital,
next to the jetty, you paced the shore
with your camera. Red gym shorts and Nike
slides, your dark hair in a low bun.
It was your job to document the beach
before its demolition, and once, in a fit of mania,
we drove out in total dark at four a.m.—
you sped past the stone church
on Flatbush, talking with your hands.
The sun rose as we stepped off the boardwalk.
We slept on blankets you kept in your car.
When we woke again, distance swimmers
were arriving by bicycle. Now at night,
outside the city, I picture the contours
of your face until they become like any other
woman's. I make myself imagine a deserted
room where people like you and I could meet.
Damp brick walls, cracked windows.
Then I remember its absence. In the end,
there is only exposure: the wind-blown recess
where a building stood.

OCTOBER PHONE CALL

I tell Meg I feel dead and she says
you're not dead you're just not in New York.
It's true, there is no music when I lock myself
inside my car, when I pay the toll to cross
the bridge and can't even see the water.
The man at the Chevron on Perkins tells me
to be happy through the slat above the register:
he says each day is a new chance to pray.
A cargo ship passes Alcatraz which is now
a museum, and in another museum, the clothes
of settlers are pinned under glass, beside
a display called Native Plants. Alone
in the Headlands on my twenty-eighth birthday,
I can see San Francisco's skyline, its treachery.
The yellow houses of Sausalito. Bunkers
filled with beer cans built into the hills.
For a decade, my entire childhood, my father
photographed an abandoned copper refinery
in Brooklyn. I sat by the river and watched him.
My loneliness is not less because I understand
it more, or because I have condoned it. Mist
and roads in all directions. Is this an ending.
What about now.

IF ANY PLOT CLOSES

Sunlight struck the dangerous metal objects
in the kitchen. Knife and coffee grinder. Blender.
Hot plate. In Southern California, all the forests
were on fire, and in Louisiana, days without electricity.
I had several belongings to retrieve from your apartment.
Someone took issue with the term Anthropocene to describe
the current climate. It would become winter. I needed my sweaters.
Ache felt primordial, like the shape left by a family member.
None of my knowledge had to do with content. My sister
sent me a video of carrier pigeons on her roof—commanded
by a whistle, the pigeons flew so beautifully together
they often made her cry. After crying, I felt thirsty.
In the mountains, I asked my friend how to live forever,
eating cherries straight from the tree. It became clear.
Romance was love with the imposition of narrative.
I saw your former boyfriend biking with no hands
and laughed manically. I considered breathwork.
I considered kumquats, the bitter taste of their skin.
Scaffolds were removed from the nearby elder home.
Someone used the word *world* as a verb. The world worlds.
There was a world inside the world. I wanted the hard pit.

AN EXPLANATION

I do not like milk. I wish I knew more children.
I am not afraid of heights. I do not fear the ocean.
I used to be the fastest swimmer, just the fastest,
out of all the girls. And once when I was twenty-one,
I hitchhiked from a rest stop in eastern Indiana
to Chicago in a logging truck. I slept
atop the trucker's backseat fold-out bed
with my cellphone and a small black knife.
At dawn he left me by the outer suburbs,
from which I called a cab directly to the doorstep
of someone else I loved, and then at twenty-three
in Lebanon, I slept alone atop a mountain,
and woke to my tent surrounded at all sides
by a sea of grazing sheep, some with bells,
their soft mouths moving by the hundreds,
and across the road two rams collided,
and the shepherd texted, and I thought
if I have a daughter I hope she's nothing like me
and from the valley came a smell of burning.

SONNET WITH TWO BRIDGES

I loved the ugly one the most. Blue and inhospitable.
My theory had to do with looking, the gaps in the chain-link
fence that we paused in front of, drunk, to stare at a passing
garbage boat, a ferry, and cars on the more famous bridge,
which could be seen west of where we stood. Soft edges,
wooden panels. I stuck my face through the wire. You placed
your hand on my waist. And we stood like that, together,
quietly unmoving, the night before you left for Philadelphia,
a landlocked city with just one river. One cracked bell.
So I guess it all comes down to water, and also elevation,
how sometimes the height of things is more honest
than the architecture. The grid and not the myth of it,
the broken fence and not the plaque. How many dawns,
wrote Crane, waiting under the pier, refusing to name his lover.

CREATION MYTH

Because a hand came out and pushed down the land.
Because a boy tried to hold two dogs together.
Because you wrote her about it. You sent a letter.
Because peacocks made cat-like sounds in the mountains,
and someone knocked twice, three times, on a smooth wooden door.
Because one's parents stared at each other on the delayed train,
gray commuters, and blood ran through a divot and bloomed,
became water spilling from the lion-mouthed fountain.
Because an impossibly large structure was built.
A pond used to exist at the edge of our city.
Mosquitos swarmed through the tall grasses.
Because one could die without knowing this,
the wild heart of all objects. In the dark, I mark myself:
One can be alive again. One can be alive ten thousand times.

NOTES

Pleasure Principle takes its title from Sigmund Freud's essay "Beyond the Pleasure Principle" (1920).

"Road to Harissa" references Dante's *Inferno*, canto 7.

"Desire Lines" takes its title from an urban planning phenomenon in which informal paths are created by human foot traffic. The poem draws upon Melanie Klein's essay "Love, Guilt, and Reparation" (1937), Jean Baudrillard's *America* (1986), and Witold Rybczynski's *A Clearing in the Distance: Frederick Law Olmsted and America in the Nineteenth Century* (1999).

"Natural History" quotes language used within a 2022 shark exhibition at the American Museum of Natural History.

"Jacob Riis Beach" takes its title from a queer beach in the Rockaways, formerly situated behind the abandoned Neponsit Beach Hospital. The Neponsit Beach Hospital was demolished in 2023.

"Sonnet with Two Bridges" quotes the poet Hart Crane's book-length poem *The Bridge* (1930).

ACKNOWLEDGMENTS

Thank you to the editors of the publications in which the following poems first appeared:

The Adroit Journal
"Provincetown"
"Voicemail from La Jolla"

American Chordata
"Natural History"

Four Way Review
"Road to Byblos"

Frontier Poetry
"An Explanation"

The Kenyon Review
"Sonnet with Two Bridges"

The Nation
"Sapphic Fragment"

Narrative Magazine
"Object Permanence"
"Inheritance"
"Narrative"
"Beirut"
"The Feast of Saint Francis"

New England Review
"At the Ashokan Watershed"

The New Yorker
"Leaving"

Third Coast
"If Any Plot Closes"

Raleigh Review and *Best New Poets*
"Creation Myth"

Virginia Quarterly Review
"Bodega Bay"
"Point Reyes"
"5 North"

Washington Square Review
"Pleasure Principle"

I've had the privilege of learning from several brilliant teachers. Here, I owe a particular thanks to two. Thank you to Shane McCrae for a decade of guidance. Thank you to Louise Glück, whose honesty and attention pushed this book toward its center. In your absence, I lack the words to describe my gratitude.

Thank you to my editor, Chris Richards, and to my agent, Rob McQuilkin, for trusting in these poems.

Thank you to the creative writing departments at Oberlin College, Columbia University, and Stanford University. Thank you to my peers at the Stegner Fellowship between 2022 and 2024.

Thank you to Carol Edgarian and Tom Jenks of *Narrative Magazine* for pivotal early support of my work.

Thank you to Jackson Holbert and Catherine Fischer, careful readers.

Thank you to the loved ones who walked with me in Brooklyn: Annie Appleweis, Joanie Cappetta, Yael Malka, Safiyah Riddle, and Leo Vartorella.

Thank you to the loved ones who welcomed me to Oakland: Will Brewer, Ryann Stevenson, Angie Sijun Lou, and Gabriel Lopez.

Thank you to my parents, Jenny Douglas and Curtis Cravens, and to my sister, Delilah Cravens.

This book is for Megan Fernandes.